Lila and Andy learn about Winter Roads

Kenneth Adams

Copyright © 2025 by Kenneth Adams
All rights reserved.

No portion of this book may be reproduced in any form without written permission from the publisher or author, except as permitted by copyright law. This publication is designed to provide general information in regard to the subject matter covered. It is sold with the understanding that neither the author nor the publisher is engaged in rendering any professional services. While the publisher or author have used their best efforts in preparing this book, they make no representations or warranties with respect to the accuracy or completeness of the contents of this book and specifically disclaim any implied warranties of fitness for a particular purpose.

Book Cover by Kenneth Adams
Illustrations by Kenneth Adams
First Edition 2025

ISBN: 978-1-998552-12-2

Knowledge is like a survival backpack. The more you pack into it, the more challenges you can overcome.

This book belongs to:

_____

Hi there! We're Lila and Andy, and we love exploring the great outdoors. Whether it's hiking up snowy mountains or watching the northern lights dance across the sky, there's always something magical to discover in winter.

Today, we're super excited to learn about winter roads! These amazing roads are built right on top of frozen lakes and rivers. Can you believe it? Cars and trucks driving on frozen water! Let's explore how these incredible roads work.

Our Dad's a structural engineer, but he's not stuck in an office all day. He works on some of the most incredible remote winter roads, and his job takes him to some of the coldest places in the world, where communities rely on frozen lakes and rivers to stay connected.

He's always telling us about the importance of ice thickness, and the different ways engineers make ice even stronger for vehicles to safely travel across.

What is a Winter Road?

Winter roads are special roads that are only used during the cold winter months. They're built when temperatures stay below freezing long enough for swamps, lakes, and rivers to freeze solid.

These roads connect communities, mines, and other remote places that don't have regular roads to the outside world. Winter roads are very important as they help move essential supplies like food, fuel, and building materials to these remote places.

A Winter Road Over Land

A Winter Road Over A Frozen Lake

Winter roads can be built over land or over the ice on frozen lakes and rivers. Many winter roads consist of both land and ice sections.

Sometimes, when the majority of a winter road is built over ice, it is also called an ice road.

In Canada, the section of land between two lakes is called a portage.

Who Needs Winter Roads?

Winter roads connect many groups of people that need reliable transportation during the cold winter months.

It takes skilled professionals working together to plan, build, and use a winter road.

Let's learn about some of the important roles involved with winter roads.

People who need winter roads include remote communities that depend on these roads to receive food, medicine, and other essential supplies.

Mining companies use winter roads to move equipment and materials to and from their mine sites, and local businesses in remote areas rely on winter roads to bring goods to their stores.

Governments and regulatory bodies are responsible for approving permits that ensure the road is built safely, respecting the environment, and the rights of Indigenous people.

<u>Engineers</u> use their knowledge of how ice and soil behave to determine the required thickness of the ice and the safest route for the road. They oversee the construction to make sure the road is built as safe as possible.

<u>Environmental scientists</u> work hard to find ways to make sure the winter road doesn't harm the surrounding environment, including plants, animals, and water.

<u>Road construction contractors</u> use special equipment to clear away snow, thicken the ice, get rid of bushes and trees, flatten the ground, and pack down snow and ice to make a smooth, solid road for driving.

Once the road is built, it needs to be maintained throughout the winter to ensure that it remains safe for use. This includes monitoring ice thickness, repairing cracks, and removing snow. <u>Road inspectors</u> make sure the road stays safe and strong all winter long.

Everyone works together to build safe winter roads, while also taking care of nature.

Winter Road Alignment

Building winter roads takes a lot of careful planning, special equipment, and hard work from very dedicated and experienced people.

Before building a road, you first have to identify the route the road has to follow. This is called the road alignment, and there are a couple of things to keep in mind when deciding where to build a winter road. It's kind of like a puzzle with lots of different pieces to think about.

First, there's the land itself. You need to consider the topography, whether there are things like hills or valleys to cross. Other things to think about are what the soil is made of, whether there are permafrost areas present, how water will drain away from the road, and if there are any obstacles or elevation changes that may affect how snow piles up on the road, or blows across the road.

The shape and depth of a lake may affect how ice forms and how strong it is!

Snow acts like a blanket and slows down ice formation on lakes and rivers.

When thinking about how bodies of water, like lakes and rivers, affect winter roads, you have to consider where they are located, how big they are, and how their water levels change throughout the year. The layout, size, and location of lakes can all affect how ice forms, how thick it gets, how strong it is, and how much you can rely on it to build a road on.

The weather can also be pretty tricky in winter. Things like which way the wind usually blows, how much sun and shade an area gets, where water from rain and snow melt is likely to flow, and how much snow may fall can all make a difference in deciding where the winter road must go.

Some animals, like caribou, use winter roads to migrate across frozen landscapes.

And don't forget about the animals! You'll need to make sure the road doesn't disturb their homes or migration routes.

You'll want to think about how much traffic the road will get, what kind of vehicles will be using it, how heavy those vehicles are, and where they're going.

We also need to think about where the water for flooding will come from, where to get construction materials like gravel from, and how to get big machines in and out for building and fixing the road.

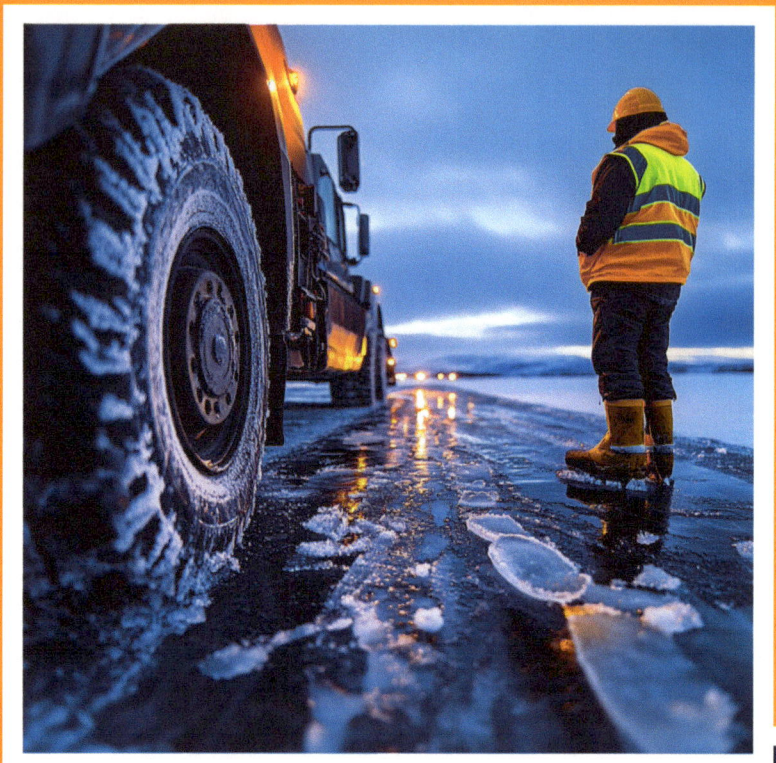

And of course, safety is always the most important thing. You want to be sure it is possible to build the road in a way that is safe for everyone.

As you can see, there are many factors to consider before deciding on where a winter road should be built. Each of these factors must be carefully considered to decide on the best and safest alignment.

Regulatory Approvals and Permits

Getting permits and approvals from the authorities before building a winter road is very important. The rules are there to keep everyone safe, protect the environment, and respect the rights of Indigenous people.

By getting the necessary paperwork in order, engineers ensure the winter road is built properly and follows all the rules, taking care of things like land use provisions and environmental protection.

Winter Road Design

 Winter roads are carefully designed to handle all the different types of vehicles that use the road. Since most winter roads are used to transport fuel, groceries, and equipment to remote locations, they have to be able to support big and heavy trucks safely.

Engineers have to keep this in mind when they design a winter road. When the road goes over land, engineers make sure the slopes aren't too steep, and that all the curves are gentle enough for long trucks to travel safely.

The road surface is also shaped so it doesn't tilt too much to either side, preventing trucks from sliding off the road or tipping over.

Winter roads over land should be about 10m wide. Snow and ice protect plant life under the road surface.

On lakes, vehicles must travel close to the centreline of the road, to avoid dangerous areas close to snowbanks.

Winter roads built on land are usually about ten meters wide. The road surface is created by using packed snow and ice. To protect plants underneath the road, it's important to make sure at least ten centimeters of snow or ice covers the natural ground.

Winter roads crossing over ice are built differently. They are designed to be at least thirty meters wide. In areas with high winds and drifting snow, the road is made even wider, to between thirty-five and fifty meters.

This extra width serves many purposes. It lowers the risk of snow drifts blocking the road during storms, and it allows for snow to be cleared off the road without making the road too narrow for trucks to pass. Trucks also have tons of room to stay far away from each other, spreading out their weight while traveling across the ice.

Special ramps of snow and ice help trucks get off the ice.

Road markers on the side of the road help drivers see the road better.

When the road changes from ice to land, engineers make sure the road is not too steep for heavy vehicles. They use snow and ice to create special ramps that make it safe for vehicles to move easily on and off the ice without getting stuck or sliding off the road.

Road markers are often placed on the side of winter roads to help drivers stay on track during snowstorms, nighttime, and other hazardous winter driving conditions.

Ice and Engineering

The most fascinating thing about water is that it behaves differently from almost everything else when it freezes. While most materials get smaller when they freeze, water actually expands and becomes less dense! That's why ice floats on water.

When a lake starts to freeze, the ice forms from the top down, not from the bottom up, since the outside air temperature is much lower than the temperature of the water. As the top layer of the water freezes, it creates a solid layer of ice that floats on the surface.

As more and more water freezes, the ice becomes thicker and stronger, and so, engineers have figured out that the floating ice can actually support weights safely. Of course, the amount of weight ice can support depends on the thickness and condition of the ice.

For example, a person walking on ice needs at least ten centimeters of thickness, while something heavier, like a snowmobile, may need twice that much. As you can imagine, the really big trucks that carry heavy loads need a lot more solid ice beneath them, in some cases even a meter or more!

A drilled hole visible through the clear, natural ice on a frozen lake.

Not all ice is the same though! Some ice is thick and strong and can support your weight. Other ice is thin and weak, and stepping on it could be dangerous.

The strength of ice can change depending on how cold it is outside, how thick the ice is, what time of year it is, and whether water is moving under the ice.

Engineers have to look out for different kinds of ice when building these amazing roads.

Clear, Solid, Blue Ice →

← White, Snowy, Broken Ice

Natural ice forms when the lake or river freezes on its own. The best kind is clear ice, which forms when water freezes slowly. Clear ice is almost transparent, which means you can see right through it since the ice is free of air bubbles. This allows light to pass through more easily, causing the blue wavelengths of light to be reflected back, making the ice appear blue.

Also known as "snow ice", white ice is cloudy and contains many air bubbles. It forms when snow is soaked with water and freezes. White ice is generally considered to be weaker and less sturdy than clear ice, and engineers try to avoid building roads over areas with white ice.

Ice being flooded to increase ice thickness

Spray ice being used to grow ice thickness

Engineers have also developed clever ways to help the ice reach the thickness needed to support weight.

One method is called <u>flooding</u>. They drill a hole through the ice, pump the water out, and let it flow onto the existing ice. This water is applied in thin layers, three to five centimeters thick, and each layer is allowed to freeze completely solid before they add the next layer. Flooding works best when it's really cold outside, say below −20°C (−4°F)!

They also use something called <u>spray ice</u>. Special machines spray a fine mist of water into the air. Once the water falls onto the existing ice cover, it freezes quickly and bonds to the ice, making the ice cover even thicker.

Spray ice is also applied in layers, and each layer is allowed to freeze completely before the next layer is sprayed on.

In both cases, during flooding and spraying, the ice is created on top of the natural ice.

When ice is created by using flooding or spraying techniques, they appear white as well, because air gets trapped in the water before it freezes.

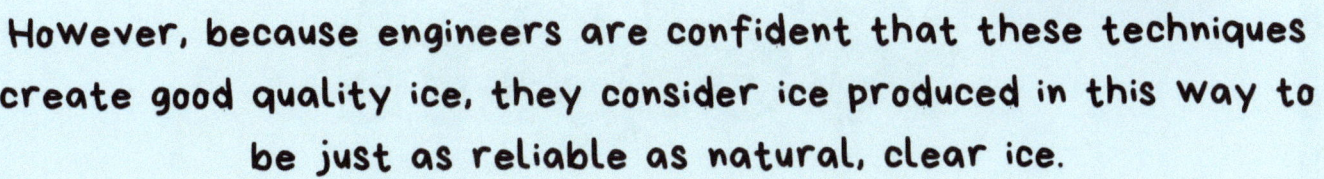

However, because engineers are confident that these techniques create good quality ice, they consider ice produced in this way to be just as reliable as natural, clear ice.

How Ice Supports Weight

Ice can support weight because of its solid structure and strength, not just because it floats. When a lake or river freezes, it forms a rigid sheet of ice on the surface. This happens because ice is less dense than water, so it stays afloat at the surface due to buoyancy.

Buoyancy is the invisible force that makes things float by pushing up on them when they are in the water. However, buoyancy alone does not determine how much weight ice can support. That depends on its condition, thickness, and strength.

The amount of weight ice can support, depends on the thickness and condition of the ice. Thicker ice is stronger and can handle more weight because it spreads the load over a larger area, however, significant cracks in the ice can make it much weaker. That's why it is so important to inspect for cracks and to check the ice thickness before driving, skating, or walking on ice.

If too much weight is added, the ice doesn't just sink, it cracks and breaks under stress. When ice breaks, the pieces still float due to buoyancy, but they can no longer support the same amount of weight as previously.

Engineers can determine how much weight ice can safely support by knowing the thickness, condition, and strength of ice. Understanding these factors helps people stay safe on frozen lakes and rivers.

Winter Road Construction

The construction of winter roads on land starts with clearing the route of all trees, bushes, and other obstacles like rocks and boulders. Once the area is cleared, heavy equipment is used to make the road level by spreading and compacting snow on the road, and then flooding it with water. When this mix of snow and water freezes, it creates a tough ice surface that can be leveled even more, providing a flat road surface for vehicles to travel on.

Building winter roads on land generally takes much longer than building them on ice. Construction can commence earlier in the season compared to building on ice, as construction equipment can be used as soon as the ground is frozen.

By drilling holes in the ice, engineers can measure the ice thickness using a special kind of measuring tape.

Construction of winter roads over ice is a relatively simple process and mainly requires the removal of snow from the ice.

Before construction equipment can be placed on the ice to clear the snow, it has to be confirmed that there is sufficient ice thickness to support the snow-clearing equipment.

An engineer measures ice thickness by dragging a GPR over the ice.

Ice thickness can be checked manually, by drilling holes and measuring it with a tape measure or measuring stick, or by profiling the ice using ground-penetrating radar (GPR).

GPR ice profiling involves dragging an antenna across the ice. This antenna sends electromagnetic waves into the ice, and when they hit the water below the ice, they bounce back up. The GPR unit records these reflected signals and uses them to create a picture of the ice thickness.

GPR profiling can quickly and accurately measure ice thickness over a large area, making it more efficient than manual methods.

SHERP amphibious vehicles are perfect for ice profiling with ground-penetrating radar (GPR) because their ultra-low ground-pressure tires can go almost anywhere. They can even float and get themselves unstuck from broken ice, which makes them super safe for ice profiling, especially when the condition and thickness of the ice are not known.

Did you know snow is actually colorless? It appears white because the ice crystals scatter light in all directions, reflecting all wavelengths of visible light equally. This scattered light makes snow look white to our eyes.

Once it is confirmed that the ice is thick enough to support the weight of the construction equipment, snow-clearing may begin.

If the ice is still too thin to allow heavy equipment on the ice, lighter vehicles like pickup trucks or all-terrain vehicles (ATVs) equipped with snow plows are used. When ice thickness is adequate for heavier equipment, contractors use plow trucks, snowcats, or graders to remove the snow.

A plow truck clearing snow along the snowbank.

The road is formed by pushing the snow to the side, exposing the bare ice. The snow forms piles called snowbanks on the side of the road.

The height of snowbanks should be controlled to allow wildlife, like moose and caribou, to safely migrate across the winter road.

Controlling the height of snowbanks also helps reduce the weight of snow on the ice, preventing cracks from appearing along the snowbank, and ensuring the safety of the winter roads.

Snow on a lake acts like a blanket, slowing down the formation of ice. Once the snow is cleared and the ice is exposed, the ice will continue to increase in thickness naturally. During this time, flooding and ice spraying can also be used to grow the ice artificially.

Keeping the Road Safe

Once a winter road is built and people start using it, it is very important to take good care of it, especially when there are ice crossings involved. Temperature changes during winter can dramatically affect the condition and thickness of ice.

A few days of mild weather can quickly weaken ice that previously seemed solid. To ensure that winter roads remain safe for use all winter long, they are continuously inspected and maintained.

Cracks in ice are a common occurrence on ice roads. Cracks form because of severe temperature changes, or because of traffic traveling over the ice.

One of the most crucial things to keep a close eye on is the ice thickness. It is important to do regular checks to make sure there are no sudden changes in the thickness of the ice over time.

Cracks forming in ice are normal as the ice expands and contracts with temperature changes. While not all cracks are bad, it could be a sign that the ice may not be safe in that area. Cracks should be fixed as soon as they appear.

It is important to do daily inspections of the winter road so cracks can be identified as soon as they form.

A clever way to fix cracks in the ice is to flood the road using water trucks. The crack is filled by the water, which freezes and seals it again.

Cracks can be fixed in a number of different ways. The easiest way is to pour water down the crack using a water truck. Once the water fills the crack, it freezes up against the ice and close the crack. Another way is to drill a hole through the crack, all the way down until you reach the water under the ice. The water from the lake will pump up into the crack and refreeze in position, closing the crack back up.

Cracks can be dry or wet. When a crack is dry, it means the crack has not yet broken through to the bottom of the ice sheet, while wet cracks are an indication that the crack runs all the way through the ice, and that water from the lake below is spilling up into the crack. Wet cracks could also show that the ice has lost some of its flotation, and is starting to sink below the water line.

To keep the winter road safe, it's necessary to frequently remove any snow on the road. Snow can make it difficult for drivers to see the road, and it can hide dangerous cracks in the ice.

Just like normal roads and highways, winter roads have speed limits to prevent accidents and keep drivers safe.

On winter roads, speed limits also have another purpose. Engineers have figured out that the speed at which a vehicle travels on ice can actually affect the condition of the ice.

A speeding truck can cause cracks to occur more frequently, or even cause blocks of ice to break out from the road surface, causing "ice potholes" in the road.

Proper road signage is also crucial for safety. Signs showing weight restrictions, speed limits, and road hazards help drivers avoid potentially dangerous situations on the winter road.

Having two-way radio communication on winter roads is also useful as it allows drivers to quickly share information about road conditions, hazards, and emergencies with other road users.

Engineers and road crews make sure winter roads stay safe all season long by performing frequent inspections and maintenance activities.

Road users can also contribute to safety by always following the rules of the road.

Taking Care of Nature

While winter roads provide crucial access to remote areas, it's important to minimize their potential environmental impacts.

Contamination of the environment is prevented by having strict rules about where vehicles can be repaired or refueled.

If any spill of contaminants occurs during the construction or operation of a winter road, it has to be properly cleaned as soon as possible.

Winter roads can affect the way animals live. Animals like caribou and moose need a lot of space to move around to find food or breed, and winter roads can get in their way.

Animals can also have a tough time because of all the noise and pollution cars and trucks cause, while water pollution can make fish sick or even kill them.

This is why it's very necessary to take special care of the land and wildlife.

Remember, never feed, chase, or injure animals when using a winter road.

The construction of winter roads on land can disturb plant life, potentially leading to changes in the way plants survive and grow. By placing a thick layer of snow and ice on the road, the plants sleeping underneath the roadbed are protected.

Winter road construction can increase sediment runoff into water bodies, affecting water clarity and aquatic life. By testing the water in lakes and rivers regularly, we can make sure it stays clean.

Climate change is having a significant impact on winter roads. As temperatures rise, the ice on lakes and rivers is forming later in the season and melting earlier, shortening the window of time when winter roads can be built and maintained. Communities that rely on winter roads find it more and more difficult to access essential services and bring in much-needed supplies like food and other resources.

In addition to shorter seasons, climate change is also causing the ice on winter roads to become less reliable. This is making it more difficult for vehicles to travel on winter roads safely, increasing the risk of accidents. As a result, many communities are being forced to use more expensive methods, like flying, to bring in groceries, clothing, and other materials necessary for their survival.

Winter Road Safety Guidelines

Using winter roads is much different from driving on normal roads, as they can be very dangerous. Here are some safety guidelines for drivers and others using winter roads.

<u>Driving Tips:</u>
- Always drive to the posted speed limits, and adjust your speed based on ice and weather conditions.
- Maintain safe spacing between vehicles, especially when on the ice.
- Allow for longer stopping distances on slippery road surfaces.
- Avoid sudden braking, acceleration, or swerving on icy surfaces.
- Use headlights, even during daylight hours, to make sure other drivers can see you, especially when driving in snowy or foggy conditions.
- Ice thickness and ice conditions can change rapidly, so stay alert for signs of weakness or cracks.
- If you're unsure about the ice thickness and ice conditions, check with local authorities or experienced guides before accessing a winter road.
- Pay attention to road signs indicating weight restrictions, speed limits, and other hazards.
- If possible, never travel alone. Always travel with another vehicle or in a convoy.
- Watch for animals crossing the road, especially at dawn and dusk.

Emergency Preparedness

- Always carry emergency provisions. Pack a winter survival kit including warm clothing, blankets, food, water, a first-aid kit, and communication devices like cellphones or inReach devices.
- Let someone know your travel plans, like where you're going, when you're leaving, and when you're expected to arrive.
- Be aware of emergency contact numbers and procedures for the area you are traveling in.
- If your vehicle breaks through the ice, try to exit the vehicle immediately and move away from the area.

Remember that winter conditions can be unpredictable, so always prioritize safety and be prepared for the unexpected.

A Great Example

One of the most significant and well-known winter roads is the Tibbitt to Contwoyto Winter Road (TCWR) in northern Canada.

When it was first constructed, it ran from Tibbitt Lake near Yellowknife in the Northwest Territories of Canada to Contwoyto Lake in Nunavut, a distance of approximately 600 kilometers.

Nowadays, it's constructed over a length of about 400 kilometers and is used to haul essential supplies like fuel, equipment, and construction materials to several diamond mines in the area.

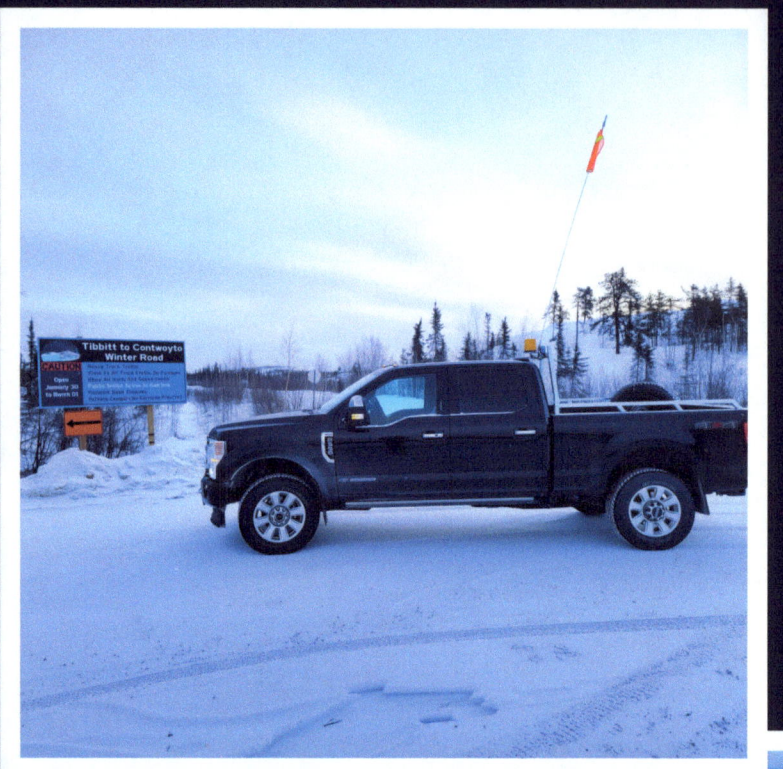

A majority of the road's length runs over frozen lakes.

Construction of the winter road starts in December and continues until late January. Depending on the weather, the road usually opens for traffic in early February and operates until late March or early April.

Construction crews stay in maintenance camps, from where they build and maintain the winter road all season long.

Engineers monitor ice conditions and thickness closely throughout the construction and use of the winter road. By understanding the make-up and weight of all vehicles using the road, engineers ensure that everyone stays safe throughout the season.

When the road reaches an ice thickness of 105cm, it can support certain trucks weighing more than 100,000kg!

Trucks carrying freight to the mines are dispatched from Yellowknife in groups or convoys for safety reasons.

Vehicle speed limits are strictly controlled, and a trip up to the mines can take almost a full day. Once there, truckers offload their cargo and immediately start the journey back to Yellowknife.

The success of the TCWR is attributed to the vast experience of the engineers and contractors who plan, build, and operate it. Their expertise in winter roads is unmatched, making this huge project possible.

Winter roads show up when we need them and disappear when spring comes. Watching these massive trucks carrying supplies safely across frozen lakes is an amazing experience. To think that in a few months, boats will be sailing right where these trucks are driving, is mind-boggling!

Now you know all about winter roads! While they might seem magical, they're actually the result of careful planning and hard work. Next time you see a frozen lake or river, remember that with the right knowledge, even frozen water can become a safe road for vehicles to travel on!

Remember to always stay safe on ice and never go onto frozen lakes or rivers without a responsible adult who knows about ice safety.

Goodbye for now, friends. Never stop learning. The world is full of wonders waiting to be discovered.

Winter Road Glossary

A glossary is like a mini-dictionary of terms with definitions.

Here's a glossary of terms used for Winter Roads.

Alignment – The planned route that a winter road follows, carefully chosen by engineers to avoid obstacles like hills, valleys, water bodies, and wildlife paths.

Amphibious Vehicle – A special vehicle that can travel on both land and water, like the SHERP.

Blue Ice – A strong, clear type of ice that appears blue due to the way it reflects light.

Buoyancy – The force that makes objects float in water. This force helps ice float and makes ice roads possible.

Clear Ice – The best type of ice for winter roads, formed when water freezes slowly with very few air bubbles. It appears blue and is very strong.

Compaction – Pressing down snow or ice to make it more solid and strong.

Construction Equipment – Large machines like snowplows and graders used to build and maintain winter roads.

Contamination – When something, like oil or gas, pollutes the ground or water.

Crack – A break or split in the ice, which can be dangerous if it spreads.

Dry Crack – A crack in the ice that doesn't go all the way through to the water underneath.

Wet Crack – A crack in the ice that reaches the water below, which may indicate sinking ice.

Drift – A pile of snow moved by the wind, sometimes blocking roads.

Engineer – A person who uses science and math to design and build things, like roads and bridges.

Environmental Protection – Rules and actions taken to keep nature safe when building winter roads.

Expansion – When ice or water takes up more space as it freezes.

Flooding – A method of making ice thicker by adding layers of water and letting them freeze.

Flotation – The ability of ice to stay on the surface of the water.

Grader – A machine used to smooth and level winter roads.

Ground-Penetrating Radar (GPR) – Special equipment that uses electromagnetic waves to measure ice thickness without drilling.

Hazardous Conditions – Dangerous situations, like thin ice or bad weather, that make winter roads unsafe.

<u>Ice Crossing</u> – A section of a winter road that goes over a frozen river or lake.

<u>Ice Pothole</u> – A hole in the ice caused by vehicle damage or natural melting.

<u>Ice Profiling</u> – The process of measuring ice thickness using tools like GPR or manual drilling.

<u>Ice Road</u> – A winter road built over frozen lakes or rivers.

<u>Ice Spraying</u> – A technique that sprays water mist onto ice to make it thicker.

<u>Load Limit</u> – The maximum weight that can safely travel on an ice road.

<u>Migration</u> – When animals move from one place to another, often to find food or have babies.

<u>Migration Route</u> – The path animals take when they move between places, which winter roads must protect.

<u>Monitoring</u> – Checking ice thickness and road conditions to keep winter roads safe.

<u>Natural Ice</u> – Ice that forms on lakes and rivers without human help.

<u>Permafrost</u> – Ground that stays frozen all year round.

<u>Portage</u> – The land section of a winter road connecting two frozen water bodies.

Ramp – A special slope built to help vehicles move safely from land onto the ice.

Regulations – Rules that must be followed to keep winter roads safe and protect nature.

Remote – A place far from towns and cities, with few people living there.

Road Alignment – The specific path chosen for a winter road.

Road Marker – Poles or signs placed along a winter road to help drivers find their way.

Safety Inspection – A careful check of ice thickness, cracks, and road conditions to ensure safety.

Sediment – Small particles of dirt and sand that can wash into lakes and rivers.

SHERP – A special amphibious vehicle that can float and travel on thin ice. It is often used for ice profiling.

Snowbank – A pile of snow along the side of the road, created when the road is cleared.

Snow Ice (White Ice) – Cloudy ice that forms when wet snow freezes. It contains many air bubbles and is weaker than clear ice.

Speed Limit – The fastest speed a vehicle is allowed to drive on a winter road.

Spray Ice – Ice created by spraying a fine mist of water into the air, which freezes when it lands on existing ice.

Thawing – When ice melts as temperatures rise.

Topography – The shape of the land, including hills, valleys, and flat areas, which affects where roads can be built.

Waterbody – A general term for any body of water, such as a lake, river, or pond.

Weight Restriction – A rule about how heavy a vehicle can be on the ice to prevent ice from breaking.

Winter Road – A special road used only in winter, often built over frozen ground or water to transport supplies to remote areas.

Winter Road Maintenance – The process of inspecting and repairing winter roads, including clearing snow, fixing cracks, and checking ice thickness.

Winter Road Safety – Guidelines and rules to ensure that vehicles and people stay safe while using winter roads, including speed limits, load restrictions, and monitoring ice conditions.

Winter Road Season – The period during which winter roads are open and safe for travel, usually from late December to early April, depending on weather conditions.

Winter Road Quiz

Multiple Choice

1. What is the primary purpose of winter roads?
    a) Tourism
    b) Scientific research
    c) Transporting essential supplies to remote communities
    d) Wildlife observation

2. When water from flooding or spraying freezes on winter roads, why does it appear white?
    a) Due to chemical treatment
    b) Because of trapped air bubbles
    c) Due to salt content
    d) Because of snow mixing

3. Which vehicle is specifically mentioned as being ideal for ice profiling?
    a) Snowcat
    b) SHERP
    c) Pickup truck
    d) Grader

4. How is ice thickness traditionally measured manually?
    a) Using sonar equipment
    b) With a laser measure
    c) By drilling holes and using a measuring stick
    d) Using electronic sensors

5. What is the recommended width for winter roads built over ice in areas with high winds?
    a) 20-30 meters
    b) 25-35 meters
    c) 35-50 meters
    d) 50-65 meters

6. What causes clear ice to appear blue?
   a) Mineral content in the water
   b) Reflection of the sky
   c) Blue wavelengths being reflected back
   d) Temperature of the water

7. Which method is used to artificially strengthen ice?
   a) Adding chemicals
   b) Electrical stimulation
   c) Flooding and spraying
   d) Mechanical compression

8. What is the primary way to check for ice safety during road operation?
   a) Weekly inspections
   b) Temperature monitoring
   c) Daily visual inspections
   d) Monthly core sampling

9. How do engineers handle the transition from land to ice on winter roads?
   a) Using metal bridges
   b) Building special ramps with snow and ice
   c) Installing floating platforms
   d) Using wooden planks

10. What environmental factor most affects ice formation speed?
    a) Wind direction
    b) Snow cover
    c) Water depth
    d) Fish activity

True/False Questions

11. Winter roads can only be built in areas where temperatures stay consistently below freezing.

12. Snow ice is generally stronger than clear ice.

13. The construction of winter roads on land takes less time than construction on ice.

14. Wet cracks in ice indicate that water from below is reaching the surface.

15. Engineers must obtain permits and approvals before building winter roads.

16. SHERPs are useful for ice profiling because they can sink through the ice safely.

17. The speed of vehicles doesn't affect the condition of ice roads.

18. Winter roads are typically built wider on ice than on land.

19. All cracks in ice roads indicate dangerous conditions.

20. Wildlife considerations are part of winter road planning and maintenance.

Fill-in-the-Blank Questions

21. The land section connecting two waterbodies in Canadian winter roads is called a _____.

22. Ice roads must be at least _____ meters wide when built over ice.

23. To protect plants underneath land-based winter roads, at least _____ centimeters of snow or ice cover is needed.

24. _____ ice profiling can quickly measure ice thickness over large areas.

25. Flooding operations work best when temperatures are below _____ degrees Celsius.

26. A _____ can form along the sides of winter roads when snow is pushed aside.

27. The height of snowbanks must be controlled to allow _____ to cross the road safely.

28. Ice forms from the _____ down, not from the bottom up.

29. Snow acts like a _____, slowing down the formation of ice.

30. When traveling on winter roads, it's recommended to travel with another vehicle or in a _____.

Advanced Multiple Choice Questions

31. What is NOT a consideration in winter road alignment?
    a) Soil composition
    b) Wildlife migration routes
    c) Summer activities
    d) Water drainage patterns

32. Which factor is most important when determining safe ice thickness?
    a) Water temperature
    b) Ice color
    c) Vehicle weight
    d) Time of day

33. What is the primary purpose of road markers on winter roads?
    a) Measuring snow depth
    b) Guiding drivers in poor visibility
    c) Marking wildlife crossings
    d) Indicating ice thickness

34. What equipment is typically used first to clear snow when ice is still thin?
    a) Heavy graders
    b) Snowcats
    c) Pickup trucks with plows
    d) Industrial snowblowers

35. Why are winter roads built wider in areas with high winds?
    a) To accommodate more traffic
    b) To allow for snow storage
    c) To prevent snow drift blockage
    d) To reduce ice stress

36. What is the best method for repairing minor cracks in ice roads?
    a) Filling with gravel
    b) Pouring water into the crack
    c) Covering with snow
    d) Adding steel plates

37. What natural process affects ice road safety most directly?
    a) Wildlife migration
    b) Temperature changes
    c) Wind patterns
    d) Precipitation

38. Which activity is NOT typically part of winter road maintenance?
    a) Snow removal
    b) Ice thickness monitoring
    c) Wildlife counting
    d) Crack repair

39. What is the main purpose of controlling snowbank height?
    a) To improve visibility
    b) To allow wildlife crossing
    c) To reduce maintenance costs
    d) To increase road width

40. What type of ice is preferred for winter road construction?
    a) White ice
    b) Clear ice
    c) Spray ice
    d) Snow ice

Advanced True/False Questions

41. Regular flooding of ice roads always makes them stronger, regardless of temperature.

42. Ground-penetrating radar can measure ice thickness without physical contact with the ice.

43. Vehicle speed limits on ice roads are solely determined by driver safety considerations.

44. White ice produced through flooding is considered equal in strength to natural clear ice.

45. Construction of winter roads can begin before the ground is completely frozen.

Advanced Fill-in-the-Blank Questions

46. When ice breaks under stress, the pieces still _____ due to buoyancy.

47. Engineers use special screens on water pumps to prevent _____ from being sucked out of lakes.

48. The thickness of flooded water layers should be between _____ and _____ centimeters.

49. Drivers should use _____ even during daylight hours on winter roads.

50. A wet crack indicates that the crack extends through the entire _____ of the ice.

Winter Roads Quiz - Answer Key

Multiple Choice Questions (1-10)
1. c) Transporting essential supplies to remote communities
2. b) Because of trapped air bubbles
3. b) SHERP
4. c) By drilling holes and using a measuring stick
5. c) 35-50 meters
6. c) Blue wavelengths being reflected back
7. c) Flooding and spraying
8. c) Daily visual inspections
9. b) Building special ramps with snow and ice
10. b) Snow cover

True/False Questions (11-20)
11. True
12. False
13. False
14. True
15. True
16. False
17. False
18. True
19. False
20. True

Fill-in-the-Blank Questions (21-30)
21. portage
22. thirty
23. ten
24. Ground-penetrating radar
25. -20
26. snowbank
27. wildlife/animals/moose/caribou
28. top
29. blanket
30. convoy

Advanced Multiple Choice Questions (31-40)
31. c) Summer activities
32. c) Vehicle weight
33. b) Guiding drivers in poor visibility
34. c) Pickup trucks with plows
35. c) To prevent snow drift blockage
36. b) Pouring water into the crack
37. b) Temperature changes
38. c) Wildlife counting
39. b) To allow wildlife crossing
40. b) Clear ice

Advanced True/False Questions (41-45)
41. False
42. True
43. False
44. True
45. False

Advanced Fill-in-the-Blank Questions (46-50)
46. float
47. fish
48. three, five
49. headlights
50. thickness

Take a look at the other subjects Lila and Andy are learning about...

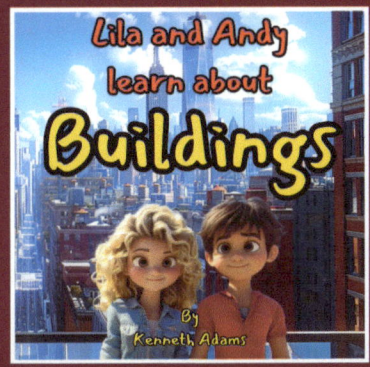

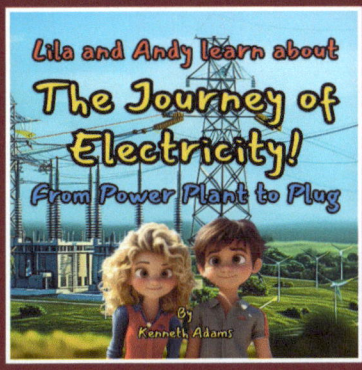
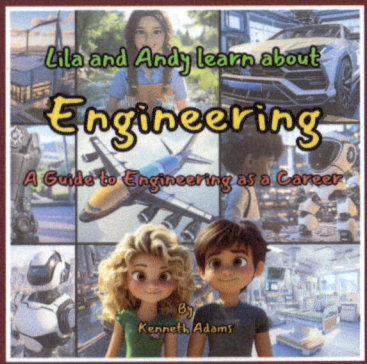
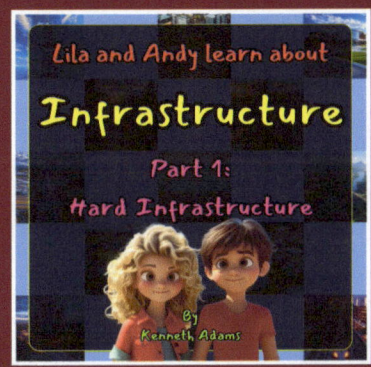
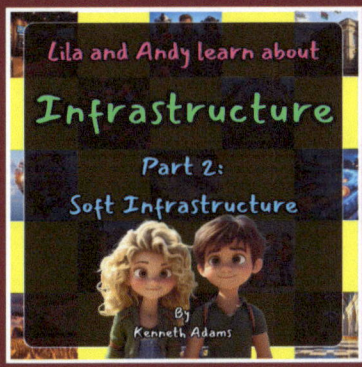
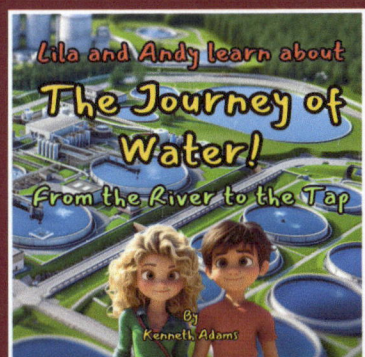
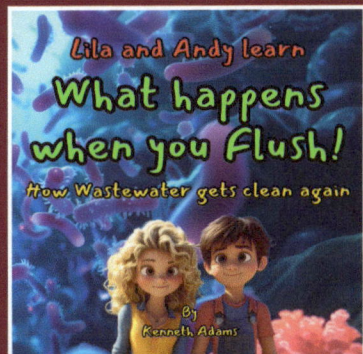
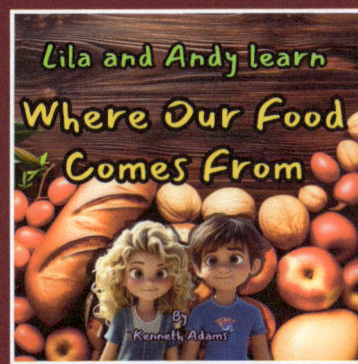
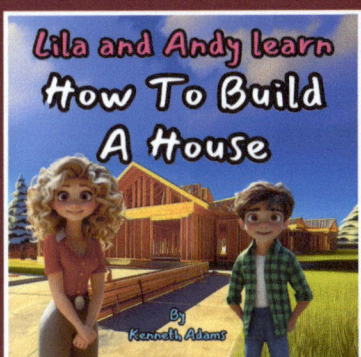
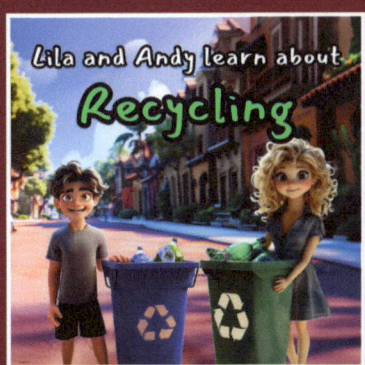

www.ingramcontent.com/pod-product-compliance
Lightning Source LLC
Chambersburg PA
CBHW042028150426
43198CB00003B/100